DEDICATION

To the woman who gave me life, taught me to never give up without a fight, the woman who has loved me like no other, to my beautiful, strong, amazing mother.

For Loretta

CONTENTS

INTRODUCTION

"This is truly a dream come true, Sharing my gift, my thoughts, and my heart with you."

-Rocky

Exposed was birthed out of a deep search of myself and the world around me. This book is proof that pain serves a purpose. I have always been such a private person that it was almost impossible for me to share this, but I've decided to expose my truth. This book gives you an intimate look into issues I have encountered, heard about, and in many cases overcome. This book was constructed with the hope that you see the world through my eyes. You are reading my mind, body, heart and soul. It is my greatest aspiration that you can identify with and be encouraged by this work. The woes of life affect us all however it is how we chose to deal with those issues that's important. Therefore, I decided to write my way through heartbreak, disappointment, depression and love in all its forms.

MIND

PERSPECTIVE

There are times I look at my life and feel I've missed the mark,

Times when I've become consumed with what appears to be falling apart,

Monumental moments I'm sure I've dropped the ball,

Been drowning in a sea of countless mistakes and paying for them all,

Seconds where I feel utterly suffocated by the fact that I've yet to reach my dreams,

Minutes where it feels I'm drifting further away from goals than it should seem,

Days when I just do not feel good enough, and it's not because I had it rough,

The truth is this pressure truly cannot be blamed on society,

Because honestly, I really am unbothered by what others perceive of me,

Nor do I go around comparing myself to anyone else,

This insurmountable pressure comes from me,

I realize that the greatness within me is worth my sheer devotion,

And if I could put other's problems down long enough to focus, I'd get that promotion,

I feel less than human when I take a genuine moment just for me,

When there are so many others who depend on me,

ROCKY THE POET

I invest in the hearts and minds of so many,

That when it's time to find the strength to encourage myself I can't find any,

I know I am worth more than the small efforts I afford myself,

And I now realize that if I don't believe in me how could I expect anyone else to?

Although I don't always feel good enough,

In the depths of my soul I know that I am,

For I was formed with greatness in mind even when I don't understand,

I was created to be much more than these minuscule moments of mistakes,

Ordained by a God who gave His life and for me, paid the highest stakes,

So, when I don't feel I'm worth it I turn to you,

Because the destiny you spoke for me, was never about me it was always about you...

I TOO HAVE A DREAM

I have a Dream that my people will stop killing each other,

And will learn to stand and fight the forces of Darkness together,

Think one day this will truly be One Nation Under God,

That my children will grow up in a world of love that's not so hard,

Oh, I have a dream today! I dream of a unified race,

One who is not judged by the color of their face,

But by the strength of their hearts,

One who stands together to face adversities instead of falling apart!

I have a dream because of you Dr. King,

I am here today because I stand on the manifestations of your dreams,

Oppressed are the minds of those afraid to dream,

Terrified to stand up, stand out, and let their light gleam,

Broken are the spirits of those who will not try,

You have told yourself you are defeated but you are living a lie,

Dominated is the personality of those who follow the lead,

Petrified to be yourself so instead their egos you feed,

You only live once, living young wild, and free these are the images
implanted in our children's heads,

But I'm here to tell you to get a grip because everyday young people are
ending up dead,

ROCKY THE POET

You only live once should mean you live life the best way possible,

That you will keep living and moving forward no matter the obstacle,

My heart aches for the youth today,

Making bad choices with no remorse and don't even know how to pray,

God is no more real to you than that tattoo on your arm,

You have no conversation with Him until you are in some sort of harm,

Other than that, you worship false idols like Lil Wayne and Nicki Minaj,

Thinking the life they live is perfect but honey that's a mirage,

Wake up and know when the devil is playing you,

Money over everything, roll up, smoke up, know what the devil is saying to you,

You only live once on this earth, yes that's true,

But when you die, you can go to heaven or hell and that is totally up to you,

You are more than poverty, greater than despair,

You are Dr. King's dream so stop living in this nightmare,

Be the Kings and Queens others died for you to be,

Walk in the Will of God and into your destiny.

THE INVISIBLE WOMAN

Who am I? I am the mother of society though I'll never be accredited that,

Although I've birth civilizations upon civilizations and carried the world on my back,

Who am I? Nothing at all to you,

Though I've fought wars and pleaded with God on behalf of you,

I have carried the weight of the entire world on my shoulders,

And given my warmth to a world that only grows colder,

Who am I? I am Queen to a very ungrateful Kingdom,

One who forgets the sacrifices I made to provide them with freedom,

Who am I? Nothing but invisible to you,

Because I'm just another "black woman," are you invisible too?

I am the forgotten, the unappreciated, the broken,

The muted, the disrespected, the unspoken,

Who am I? Another "angry black woman" they say,

Yet no one takes the time to see why I feel this way,

Or maybe they see but it's easier not to acknowledge,

All that I sacrifice daily just to give my people progress,

ROCKY THE POET

Daddy's little girl left so broken and they don't seem to understand,

It was then that I learned not to depend on a man,

Who am I? At times I don't even know,

Because no matter the love I plant in my black kings, for me His love just doesn't grow,

He chooses anyone other than the sister to his struggle,

He can't see the bigger picture because he leaves behind the heart of the puzzle,

I am a beautiful enigma and I'm fine with that,

And because they fear what they don't understand they try to attack,

Who am I? Nothing more than a booty call to you,

Good enough for the night but becoming your wife will never do,

Though it is my womb that has given life to generation after generation,

Yet here I stand fighting my own brothers for desegregation?

Even handicapped by life,

I still find a reason not to give up the fight,

Who am I? I am the God-appointed lover of your soul,

Yet loving me back isn't even a goal,

I am the one being slaughtered by the ones I protect,

EXPOSED: MY WRITE TO LIVE

The constant target of blatant disrespect,

I am the fed up, the disgusted,

The loyal one who is most mistrusted,

Who am I? I am her, and I carry grief no one cares to understand,

An invisible warrior waging war and forever taking a stand,

Far from a punk yet humbly trying to survive,

Containing my strength just enough to keep hope alive,

I am perseverance in its most natural state,

Search all you want but I cannot be replaced,

Who am I? I am a daughter to the King of everyone,

I am the vessel He chose to give life to His Only Son,

I am a Black woman and I will not be ignored,

I am a Queen and no matter my tribulations I am still worth fighting for,

I am the quiet storm that changes the atmosphere,

The one who sees you down and out and won't just leave you there,

Who am I? Despite your efforts to break my spirit I am still a Queen,

Standing here motivating my sisters to follow their dreams,

Every breath I take is a glorious reminder that I am free,

That no matter the evils I face I cannot allow it to ruin me,

But as they say, "To thine own self be true,"

I know who I am, but the question is who are you?

WHEN THE DREAM GIRL WAKES UP

How do you sleep on your dream girl?

You rather be nothing to her when you were my whole world,

How do you kill me when you were my whole life?

How can you rob yourself by cheating on your own wife?

I just want to look at you without the pain,

I feel like I got murdered by someone with the same name,

After all we were supposed to be one,

So how do you cheat while I carry your unborn son?

Why? Why play the woman that only wants the best for you?

The woman who'd do anything she can for you,

But the truth is I'm not even mad at you, I'm mad at myself,

Because against my better judgment I trusted you more than anyone else,

You made a fool out of me and I willingly let you,

You took full advantage of the way that I loved you,

If I could go back and start all over again,

I would go back and never press send,

ROCKY THE POET

I hate the person pain has turned me into,

And I hate myself for still loving you,

Maybe I should cheat too,

Then you can understand how it feels when your best friend betrays you!

I don't even feel connected to you anymore,

Every day I'm wondering what am I still fighting for?

What's so wrong with me that your love has forsaken me?

When I gave everything, I had in its entirety,

And it still wasn't enough for you!

You're an idiot yet I feel like the fool,

And I hate how you try to bring stuff up as if it even compares,

Just because you don't want to hear it, I get it, I'm completely aware!

So, the best thing to do,

Is just let completely go of you,

You slept on your dream girl and it's not fair,

Now we are both woke living in this nightmare.

Cardi B said be careful with who you're choosing,

You may want to consider if what you gain is worth what you're losing?

If being the man in these streets is worth destroying your home?

EXPOSED: MY WRITE TO LIVE

If attention from random girls is worth being alone?

Be careful with me because I'm not what you're use to,

You don't see that killing me brings death to you?

You're playing Russian roulette with the realest one on your team!

How do you even aim your gun to fire shots at your Queen?

Be careful with me because I'm your best gift yet!

And if I were you, I wouldn't want the gift giver upset!

Yeah, she may be bad and she may be fine,

But she is a dime a dozen Me, I'm once in a lifetime!

MY STORY

Picked up the book of my life and began flipping through the pages,

Couldn't help but smile as I noticed the many changes,

Lord You brought me a mighty long way and I'm so grateful,

The tears that filled my eyes are only because I'm forever thankful,

He picked me up every time I fell and never stopped loving me,

He spoke to my destiny even while others were judging me,

Chapter after chapter one thing remained the same,

Lord you were always there whenever I called on your name.

TRUTH IS

The struggles of a BLACK MAN are often overlooked,

We have become NOTHING MORE than the statistics you read about in books,

But you don't take the time to know us nor hear our side,

We were born into a world of takers, FOR US there were no free rides,

I hustled to feed my family, what's the politicians excuse?

But me, you lock up for the max, while others walk away from child abuse,

I served my time and came out ready to be a NEW MAN,

BUT my past interferes with my future because no one understands,

I can't explain to them that the nigga I killed, killed my lil brother,

Nor that I sold drugs because me and my siblings ain't have no mother,

Yes, the struggles of BLACK MEN are often misconstrued,

I'm not making excuses for the woe is me attitude,

I'm just saying I want to do right,

But for everything I get in life, I have to fight,

I want my children's life to far exceed my own,

To show my son that killing, and slanging don't make you grown,

But when times get hard the streets do call,

Praying to God that this time I don't fall,

ROCKY THE POET

They tell me to go to school but that don't pay the bills,

Struggling daily with God's Will...

I'M NOT YOUR LITTLE SECRET

So, you say you want to be my friend,

You would like to get to know me,

Yet this is done in private and not openly,

Oh, I'm sorry you would like to be discreet,

Telling me lavish stories of how you'd sweep me off my feet,

You are in my inbox with elaborate depictions,

But your girlfriend you seem to forget to mention,

Please let's stop this silly charade,

I am a veteran at this game being played,

I take no pleasure in what it is you are trying to do,

I was once that girl you are hurting, so I have no respect for you,

No, now hear me out, as I have listened to your views,

Allow me to make this perfectly clear, if I'm not friends with your girl, I have no use for you,

Now we can do a group chat and discuss this if you'd like,

Because I'm a grown woman and I have no desire to fuss nor fight,

Especially over a man I could truly never call my own,

So as you stated "I'm a beautiful Queen" and I'll patiently wait for the King of my Throne!!!

FOOL ME ONCE

Pay close attention to the ones who step up,

When you decide you have had enough,

If that is the only time you notice a change,

But shortly after things remain the same,

Dump the pretender because that's all it is,

People playing games like little kids,

But if they make the change and keep it up,

They know your value and hope to change their luck,

They've seen your worth and pictured life without you,

Decided that's not how they want to live and are willing to work for you,

But see clearly and do not be fooled,

Make sure that all of their cards have been pulled,

Leave no room for trickery or mess,

Put their words to the test,

Actions speak louder than words yes this is true,

But until now they have also acted like a fool,

Never ask someone to change for you because that won't work,

They will end up lying to you and looking like a jerk,

Simply state what you want and stand your ground,

Leave it to them to make the change if they want you around.

LETTER TO MY SISTERS

Dear sister of mine,

Please listen with your heart and not your mind,

Hear my love while there's time,

See I'm not here to condemn you,

Nor am I here to cast any judgment on you,

I come simply to say you don't have to face the same mess as others before you,

I want to tell you, you're beautiful,

So, you don't have to take half-naked selfies to feel it, as some insecure ritual,

Know that your beauty radiates from the soul,

So, let your spirit speak with a truth that owns you,

Let your attitude and your behavior reflect a more regal you,

Hoe, Thot, Slut, Bitch, how could these words ever define you?

Rise above the video vixen mentality,

Show them the Queens we were predestined to be,

Designed by God to reign,

Never to succumb to disrespect or being called out your name,

Be secure in knowing you and elegance are one and the same,

My sister, you are made by God and He is pleased,

EXPOSED: MY WRITE TO LIVE

He loves your big hips, your thick hair, you don't need a weave,

You never need any false extremities,

Dear sister you are not valued based on the size of your behind,

I wish you knew the power of your mind,

I pray you'll believe in yourself and support your own shine,

I encourage you to find genuine love for yourself,

And stop glorifying the bodies of someone else,

Please, please learn the difference between riches and wealth,

Because our daughters need our help,

Be the type of woman you'd want to raise, take ownership of your future and stop passing days,

And every chance you get encourage another sister and sing her praise,

See many won't read this because it's far too long,

But can recite for you with passion every word to the Flawless song,

And you may disagree and say I'm wrong,

But one thing's for certain, one thing I know to be true,

You can never use the excuse, that no one ever told you,

And I vow not to be the one nor will I allow others to speak negatively about you...

REVERSE

So here I am, I finally made it, truly living my dream,

Only to be smacked in the face with the reality that I still have yet to find my Queen, Countless dates and too many failed relationships,

After all the promotions, awards, houses and cars who knew it'd end like this?

Staring at the body I worked hard to achieve,

While it attracts great attention, they all seem to leave,

Funny because by anyone's standards I have it all,

But what does it matter to have the world to share and no one to call,

No one to miss you or check to see if you're okay,

Hell, the only time I hear from them is when they have a bill they want me to pay,

Crazy because you can work so hard to create a wonderful life,

And it still won't give you half the happiness of finding a good wife,

See I didn't know that I was doing this all for her,

She gives me the motivation to fight harder and trust that I'll always conquer,

Her, She, I don't even know who she is,

But Lord I promise if you just send her, I'll give her the best I have to give,

I'll love her as You loved the church,

EXPOSED: MY WRITE TO LIVE

We will love each other pass the hurt,

It's crazy how all I hear is how women want a good man,

But yet here I am single because they can't see beyond dollar signs; I just don't understand,

They don't see me for who I am,

All they see are material things; they don't care about the man,

And there is no way I can ever be with a woman like that,

Because when it's all gone, she won't have my back,

So, I guess I choose to be single because I rather wait on my Queen,

Then to be stuck with just another sexy wet dream,

If she doesn't have substance, she can't have me,

She has to be beautiful far beyond just what the eye can see,

She has to be offering all of the above,

Because she must meet me at the standards of my love,

Dear Queen if you are reading this,

Know that your King is patiently waiting to give you this,

A life and love you never have to question,

A lifetime of loyalty that'll never have you guessing,

I'm not looking for perfection, just be perfectly you,

Because there is so much I plan to be, and I simply can't, without you.

I CAN'T BREATHE

I can't breathe! Suffocated by others perception of me!

Stifled by false hopes of nasty reality!

Choking on the facts that no one accepts me!

Asphyxiated by what they would have me to be!

And I can't breathe! I'm out of air completely!

Everyone is consumed with self and no one cares about me!

Devastation at this point would be a reprieve!

Because when I speak they refuse to believe!

My point of view they decline to see! Instead they rather slay me!

Kick me when I'm down and it's frustrating!

Because I CAN'T BREATHE! And I can't seem to get up!

I'm so tired Lord and enough is enough!

I'm trying to be humble but I ain't no punk!

Nothing comes easy in life but why it gotta be so tough!

All of this pressure, MY GOD I'm bout to bust!

Because I CAN NOT BREATHE! And yet you stand and watch me die!

Broken into pieces and left alone to cry!

Why do I have to work overtime just to get a fair try,

Just to be seen, as non-threatening,

EXPOSED: MY WRITE TO LIVE

I have to give up my culture and embrace their dream,

I'm defeated before I start and guilty before I act it would seem,

Stretched beyond my limits because I CAN NOT BREATHE!

Not one breath, while the life is being choked right out of me,

At the same time you stuff down my throat your views of equality,

Saying I'm racist while you recite the same thoughts as the Nazi's,

It's not that you're blind more like you refuse to see,

That you are killing me because I can't breathe...

WHITE NOISE

If there were anything I hated,

It would have to be the radio, an array of sounds,

That weigh me down,

With empty beats and lyrics with nothing to say,

Floating in thin air around my head,

With no direction or message to relay,

Yes I've grown to hate the radio,

In a world full of poetry I find myself quite out of place,

These words are not poetry but rather a disgrace,

There is no art coming from those that identify themselves as artists,

They tickle ears and entertain, but the heart and mind they miss,

Noise that doesn't inspire, doesn't admire, doesn't motivate,

Echo's not of love but actually sound more like hate,

Hate that word again, but did I mention, that I also hate TV,

Proverbial reality shows with the same story as the next,

Who is sleeping with who, and who is whose ex,

Vile creatures dressed to impress,

No heart, no morals, but given a platform for their mess,

EXPOSED: MY WRITE TO LIVE

Man I hate TV, for all it's come to be,

One in every room to keep us separate but equal,

While we rush apart to catch a stupid reunion sequel,

Family time lost in cable with infinite channels,

So we know less about each other than we do celebrity panels,

I demand we bring back the times and we recreate the days,

We develop less garbage and more Marvin Gaye's,

We worry less about shaking our behinds and more about life,

Creating less sex and more love promoting husband and wife,

Not hoes and niggas, Nor how you took a key to make six figures,

I love life, I love beauty, I love positivity,

I hate the things that kill these daily.

LOST KINGS

Brothers, cousins, friends,

Kings of all titles, Black men,

If no one told you, King you need to protect your seed,

Because uncared for children and baby momma drama you just don't need,

It is time for you to wake up,

You should now be passed just getting your nut,

But what you can't keep doing is blaming her,

When you willingly gave your seed to her!

It's no one's fault but your own if you have children you can't see,

When you decided to have sex with a woman who lacks maturity,

You pay loads of child support and have nothing to show,

Because you just had to have sex with a "hoe",

You were in love with the cat so much so you never stopped to realize,

That the woman connected to the vagina would actually be your demise,

Just like you don't want a woman that's done everything with everybody guess what Sir, neither do we!

I'm not here to throw shade my brother, just here to provide clarity,

It is beyond time for you to hold yourself in higher regards, where is your self-esteem,

EXPOSED: MY WRITE TO LIVE

Your dick shouldn't be more precious to you than what it seems,

But above all of that Kings, you have got to protect your seed,

That is your lineage, your legacy, your contribution to society,

So why are you freely giving it to just anyone?

Make them earn the right to give birth to your son!

It is time we stop making excuses and start making better decisions,

Stop letting our sons run wild while our daughters have to ask for permission,

Kings it is time for you to learn to wait on your Queen,

Instead of investing in those who just want to be seen,

Boys will be boys is now played the heck out,

Stop planting your seeds among weeds because you can't pull out!

TIRED

I'm tired, I'm tired of lies and phony friends,

I'm tired of wack tv and even wacker men,

I'm exhausted with being nice when I really don't want to,

I've had it with being politically correct to people who don't give a damn about you,

Yes I'm good and tired,

Tired of empty phone calls that leave me uninspired,

Tired of people who much too often take my kindness for granted,

Tired of idiotic emergencies that leave my life frantic,

I'm over people who can't see the mess they create,

I've had enough of people abusing love and causing hate,

I AM TIRED! I'm fed up,

With those who feel they can hurt others because they are down on their luck,

I'm sick of the way this world laughs at those who are hurting,

And disgusted by those "they" feel are more deserving,

I'm tired of the lack of respect that goes on around me,

Tired of the sickness that seems to surround me,

EXPOSED: MY WRITE TO LIVE

Tired of cancer and all the ways it affects us,

Tired of wishing for better in a sea of negativity that connects us,

I'm tired of crappy parents who don't know how to raise kids,

Sick of hearing "Hey, you gotta get it how you live," I'm exhausted with stupidity,

I'm over the blind who can see perfectly,

I'm done with the deaf who have no problems hearing,

I'm burnt out with those who are nothing like how they are appearing,

I'm Tired!!! I'm through with jokes that embarrass us as a race,

Sick of the blatant disrespect and disgrace,

I'm tired of being tired, and sick of being pissed,

I'm tired of love not lasting and yet we continue to take the risk,

I'm tired of broken promises and living nightmares,

I'm tired of folks who tell your business while pretending to care,

I'm tired of people cheating and being dumb,

I'm sick of side chicks who think they've actually won,

I'm just done, I'm over it all,

I'm tired of important things that others try to make small,

I'm tired of writing for lazy people who won't read,

People who won't support unless you are a celebrity, I'm tired of being tired,

So I live, I write, to try to inspire,

All of you who feel like I do,

Who are also very, very TIRED TOO!!!

STRANGERS

You do realize that I don't know you,

And yet how can this be possible when half of me is you,

How is it that we share blood and not memories?

They say that everything that glitters ain't gold, but you weren't even shimmery,

You didn't even give me one solid year,

You've never wiped away a single tear,

And yet the truth is that I'm not even mad,

Because how can you miss what you never had,

Expected to adjust to this giant hole,

Because my father-daughter bond you stole,

You decided that life had more to offer without me,

You never even spent one birthday with me,

I wonder when you're alone what goes through your mind,

Do you ever wish you could turn back the hands of time?

Do you recognize the heartache I faced?

Being the child of a stranger feeling so out of place,

Being so full of anger and not really knowing why,

Trying to find acceptable reasons why you just wouldn't try,

ROCKY THE POET

Why you were never there, why you just couldn't care,

Or why can't I hate you!

Because no matter the anger or the fact that we're strangers I'm still apart of you...

BLENDED PAIN

I don't think I could ever understand,

Hurting your kids to get back at a man,

I know you can't see through the pain,

And maybe that's what's causing you to get out of your lane?

Maybe that is the motive for you acting so crazy,

Or why you constantly feel the need to disrespect me,

I have been where you are sis,

And still never would I ever act like this,

I have been called out of my name by women whose children I genuinely love,

Trying to hold on to my integrity while they push, and they shove,

Fighting to protect innocent children from the nonsense of their own mothers,

Because love doesn't expose it covers,

I don't want my kids to be subjected to this,

Yes, I said my kids, we share the same name get over it,

I wanted to be an ally and build a bond to build up these kids,

You want to tear down everything and cause chaos where I live,

You waged war on my entire family trying to get even with a man,

ROCKY THE POET

In doing so you hurt your own child, but that you don't comprehend,

You are so busy running after child support that you fail to see,

Exactly who is caring for your child sweetheart, ME!

It's me who covers the deficit while you constantly take,

It's me trying to speak life to your child while you demonstrate hate,

It's my kids who suffer when you keep them away,

My God I hope you really get it one day,

I just don't get how you can be rude,

To the woman who makes sure your daughter's hair is done so you don't have to,

How can you allow bitterness to make you blind?

And not be grateful or thankful it blows my mind,

How can you take advantage of an entire family?

I truly don't know how in the world you could have a problem with me?

But it is yours to be had,

And it's really quite sad,

It's like you expect me to bow down to you,

When the truth is, I owe your kids I don't owe you,

And they get all of the love I could possibly give,

And are taught about character and the right way to live,

EXPOSED: MY WRITE TO LIVE

So, no, I will never understand,

Hurting your own kids to get back at a man,

And I won't ever hate you,

But instead will always pray for you,

Pray that one day you will see,

That the enemy you face is within, it isn't me!

BODY

WORK OF ART

I am a perfectly messed up piece of art,

Every smudged line is exactly right,

Splattered all over the canvas of life,

Dried up old paint fingerprinted with my past,

Embedded deep within the picture frame to keep me humble,

You can see where my creator has been working on me,

For I am a perfectly messed up piece of art,

Traces of old pencil marks where I attempted to erase,

Covered by bright hues of better days,

The color of love seen throughout this piece,

The Artwork forever known as "Me"

I'D RATHER RESCUE MYSELF

I'm a hell of a Woman so who do you think you're speaking to?

Walking around with your pants down calling me out my name just won't do,

I'm a hell of a Woman as if I have to explain,

So it takes much more than wine and grind for me to give up my last name,

I'm a hell of a Woman so you better check yourself,

I have rocked the world in my arms and loved harder than anyone else,

Yes men may lead nations,

But they wouldn't be there if not for my persuasions,

I'm one hell of a Woman so be reminded when you approach me,

That it takes a hell of a man to truly captive me!

I wish I was all butterflies and fairytales but that's not the life I lead,

Instead I am the rose that bloomed through concrete,

I was never daddy's little princess though I demand the respect of a Queen,

I live in reality so I'm not impressed with the Man of my "dreams,"

Gentle and delicate? Nope not her,

I rather give you the ugly truth and that's what I prefer,

EXPOSED: MY WRITE TO LIVE

I'll admit I've been called a thug,

Because I can be ruthless when it comes to protecting the ones I love,

I don't sit around waiting for Prince charming to rescue me,

I am more than capable to save myself from any emergency,

I'm a Hell of a Woman full of strength I'm no one's damsel in distress,

I need no fairytale ending to bring me happiness,

I can kill my own dragons and fight my own battles,

This woman was built tough so she's not easily rattled,

True loves kiss can kiss my behind,

Because FYI Prince Charming I'm doing just fine!

RANDOM MOMENTS

We caught eyes as he walked past,

Breaking the gaze we both kinda laughed,

Intoxicating fragrance grasp my attention as he walked by,

Stops me in my tracks, I can't speak as if I'm shy,

I search my brain to find any word to say,

He smiles a glorious smile that only furthers the delay,

I hear my brain yelling at my lungs to breathe,

My lungs can barely hear over the loud sound of my heart beat,

But they comply and I inhale a gulp of his scent,

The words I finally found once again had went,

We stood in silence for what seemed like hours,

Before he broke it asking me if the rose was my favorite flower,

I looked puzzled I suppose,

He pointed to the tattoo my shirt had exposed,

I smiled and finally said yes,

He smiled back and again I was a mess...

MY VOICE

I've been told I talk loud, which sometimes is surprising to me,

Because for so long I was the girl with no voice, forced to sit quietly,

Forced to be someone else, other than who I was created to be,

Now wait let me pause because sometimes I went willingly,

Just to keep fools close to me,

Though loving them was killing me,

Though pleasing them meant denying me,

Though I bit my tongue subconsciously,

I was a roaring lion demanding to be seen, and so I talk loud,

When really you mistake the tone because I just think I'm speaking proud,

Speaking with passion because I have an opinion and now I'm not afraid to share,

I have something to say rather you listen or not I don't really care,

I'm beyond asking and ventured into taking what's fair,

Therefore, I talk loud,

Because up until this moment I've attempted to play nice,

Up until this moment I really didn't want to fight,

Up until this moment I allowed you to dim my light,

But then you began to refuse sight,

ROCKY THE POET

You began to confuse wrong from right,

And so, I had to talk loud, I had to speak up,

I could no longer ignore the perpetual nagging feeling in my gut,

Telling me to love who I am even tho at times it would seem you don't give A...,

Yea I had to speak up,

Stand up for myself and speak on my own behalf,

Speak to my future and kill my past,

Talk passed the hurt until I am able to laugh,

Because if I do not speak you will feel my wrath,

So yes, I talk loud...

ROLE THE DICE

She is the sexiest thang in school,

She does what she wants she doesn't follow the rules,

My boys been sweatin her, yea she a ten,

Tryin to get her to come over so we can get it in,

I get her over to my crib and I'm hopin' she goes,

I'm touchin' all over her she ain't sayin' no,

I tell her that I gotta get a condom but she beggin' me to stay,

Your boy super happy because I'm going raw today,

She did it better than it's ever been done,

Yea we bout to be on and have some fun,

Except a week later I found out she's deceased,

Because she didn't tell anyone that the virus had increased,

Now I'm sittin here scared out of mind and filled with rage,

But it'd be no one's fault but my own if I got AIDS....

MY ROOTS

I went to sleep and woke up in the Harlem Renaissance and the poems of Claude McKay,

I could barely contain myself and couldn't find the words to say,

As Zora Neale Hurston then takes the stage,

I look over at Langston Hughes who seems so engaged,

As she finishes her story the Jazz starts to play,

And I am awestruck by the voice of Billie Holiday,

Dancing with Langston, nothing could go wrong,

Then I hear the glorious sounds of Mr. Armstrong,

He played for hours we danced, and we laughed,

Oh, to be a woman of this marvelous past,

The way We spoke, the way We dressed,

The pride that We carried, the love We expressed,

It was so beautiful I couldn't stop my tears,

Then the alarm clock goes off and "Mommy I'm hungry," is all I hear...

EXTRAORDINARY

Normally I would hide myself behind jokes and laughs,

Normally I'd be too ashamed to admit I was trapped by the pain of my past,

Normally I'd push you away, while I pulled away too,

Normally I'd want nothing to do with you,

But please don't take offense to what I just said,

Because normally my relationships haven't been spirit led,

Normally I don't speak first, normally I'd just wait,

But when God spoke up I knew it had to be fate,

When a real man enters your life, I figured I better take this chance,

So normally I don't stare, normally I barely even glance,

So, forgive me for being rude,

And please be understanding when I seem distant trust, it's no attitude,

It's just that I want to fall in love with you,

But that has been painful so at the same time I don't want to,

Normally I can't look at someone and see them the way I see you,

Normally I don't think of them the way I think of you,

I hate to admit I'm in love with your eyes,

Because when you look at me it is the truth there's no lies,

ROCKY THE POET

I can't stand that I'm in love with your face,

And the fact that I feel like I can't go a day without your embrace,

Because normally this is just some crap I wouldn't do,

Normally I could stop myself from falling for you,

But this ain't normal, this is so different,

Normally guys are deaf to me while you, well you listen,

So at times I want to run because this scares me,

But I can't because there is nowhere else I'd rather be,

Than right here staring at you, giving you all of me...

FACING MY FEARS

I rub the scars on my body as I remember,

Exactly what happened to cause them last November,

Tears fill my eyes as I recall, the night I took that terrible fall,

The day I took that horrendous leap,

To tumble out of promises that were never meant to keep,

The moment I fell from cloud nine,

Plummeted to near death only to discover I was fine,

Though the scars are still present, the wounds did heal,

You stole blood, sweat, and tears from me but never took my will,

Bones were never broken though my heart was shattered,

I collected the pieces and realized you never mattered,

Yes, I touch the scars you left, and my eyes fill with tears,

But tears of joy because I was able to face my fears...

CAN YOU SEE ME?

The constant reference to my color, at times has annoyed me,

Because I'm assumed to be this person based on false concepts of reality,

Biased opinions developed over time with no real validity,

Created with hate as the motive and no sound sincerity,

The constant reference to my color, at times has made me mad,

Because there has been opportunities snatched away that with all rights I should have had,

The fact that I'm assumed to be a single mother,

Or a lazy brother makes me sad,

Because I'm just an angry black woman when I have every right to be mad,

The constant reference to my color, at times is expected,

Because you are unfamiliar with my struggle and how in darkness I was perfected,

Or how I learned to encourage myself when I felt neglected,

You don't recognize my past so my present isn't respected,

The constant reference to my color, at times breaks my heart,

The fact that it comes from those with the same background is the hardest part,

Because we've shared the same blood from the start,

So how is there levels, dimensions, or hierarchies between us just because I'm light and your dark?

BIOLOGICAL CLOCK

I hear the clock ticking loudly and I just want it to shut up,

Who cares that I'm over 30, single, and down on my luck,

As I stare in the mirror, I don't recognize the woman looking back at me,

She is beautiful, strong, independent, and alone yet not lonely,

I thought for sure I'd be married by now,

I'd have a house, a child, and be perfectly settled down,

Ha what a joke there is no man in sight,

Even after I stopped hoping for Mr. Perfect, and was settling for Mr. Right,

What do I need to change, hmmm I often contemplate,

Should I cut, color, or grow my hair, maybe lose some weight,

But then I say bump that those things don't define me,

A real man will not care he will love me for me,

But I want a baby or my own to hug and kiss,

One to have my face, his name, and fill my every wish,

So yes, your deceitful clock I hear ticking,

However, I am 30, single, and still fabulously winning.

HEART

FOR NANA

You gave me lessons I carry in my spirit every single day,

Though at the time I didn't understand the message you were trying to relay,

You were the first person to speak abundant life to me,

You told me that I would be a model but there was so much more than outward beauty,

You told me I would be a lawyer and to stand up for what's right,

You played with me when I cried at night,

You let me play in your make-up and clothes,

All while allowing me to give you my childhood woes,

Man were you Beautiful, I often mimic your pictures,

When I'm in a funk I can still hear your whispers,

"Roxanne smile because you are too pretty to frown,

God is too good for you to allow the devil to bring you down,"

Loved by many but adored by me,

Thank you, Nana, for implanting a Woman in me,

That I was once too young to see,

I was seven when you left but I held on to that love,

I hope to make you proud while you are watching from above,

Happy Birthday, you are still a present thought in my mind,

Thanks to your love and kindness we are all doing just fine.

FOR MY MOM AND DAD

Mom I never knew your struggles, but I know you gave your best,

Did things for our giggles and to bless us with happiness,

As I now walk your path I can truly see,

That loving us despite our wrong wasn't always easy,

Who compares to God, there is no other,

But to help show His love He gave us all mothers,

The wisdom you often share,

No life lesson could compare,

You have given your all and I'm grateful for that,

I know I can go on because you have already proven that,

The love I have for you far exceeds these words,

Thank you for standing up for me when I didn't have the nerve,

Thank you for all you did and still do,

That is why I dedicated this book to you,

There isn't a day that I don't thank God for you,

Going above and beyond for me even when you don't have to,

You have loved me from day one that much I know,

You have encouraged and strengthened me to help me grow,

You are in a class all your own and quite unique,

You are a man with a sword for a tongue and yet that part I'll still keep,

You love me with your whole heart even though I share no blood with you,

And I'm grateful because out of all the men God could have sent my mom, He chose you!

LETTER TO MY DAUGHTERS

Dear beautiful, there is so much I want to let you know,

So much I have to say, so much for you I pray,

I choose to live my life in a way that you can relate to,

So that you can look at me and see the same beauty in you,

I don't wear weave, nails, or eyelashes,

Because I want you to trust that you are already perfect as time passes,

I don't want you to see me glorifying anything that is fake,

Nor do I want you to grow up finding parts of yourself to hate,

Therefore, I must live by example and be the woman I want to see in you,

I can't carry myself in a manner that goes against what I'm trying to teach you,

I have made many mistakes that I will always be open about,

So that you can make better decisions for your life and never have to live in self-doubt,

I get up when I want to stay down, smile when I want to cry,

Just to show you to never give up without a try,

I push forward and love myself every day,

Because I'm aware you are paying attention to everything I do and say...

FOR OUR SONS

Baby boy as you sit in my lap, I just want to protect you,

Protect you from a world that is unfair to you,

Handsome child of mine, I pray God covers you and keep you in line,

How do I tell you, how do I explain?

That you can't go out in the world and behave the same,

How do I tell you race doesn't matter, we are all equal,

When a white man can kill you and be called a hero,

How on earth do I tell you to be mindful of your skin,

But then turn around and explain the enemy within,

Do I tell you that you will always be judged on what you look like?

And watch the confused look on your face as you tell me it's not right,

Baby boy I love you, right now you're too young to understand,

That in this country a dog's life is worth more than a Black man,

How do I help you find your worth, while the world decided you're worthless?

So, I take a stand to push your God-given purpose,

Son don't let your perception be jaded by the scum of the earth,

Remember that you are always a blessing and never a curse,

The devil longs to take out our Black man,

ROCKY THE POET

But baby boy hold on to God's unchanging hand,

Believe the love I have always shown you,

Not the self-hate that is forced on you,

Trust in the Lord with all your heart and do your best,

And rest assured God will take care of the rest,

Trust Him and not our system it was not designed with us in mind,

Know yourself and where you come from and the truth, you'll always find...

WHISPERS OF A BROKEN HEART

Your words on repeat in my brain,

As I play and replay the pain,

Words that you said with such confidence, that strolled out of your mouth and left me broken,

Words that danced on my confidence and killed any words I could have spoken,

You ever been so hurt by something someone said, all you could say was WOW,

I mean like these vile words seemed less like a hateful lie and more like a vow,

I mean like they dug deep in their soul to find the right bomb to drop on you,

And even though you sit knowing it's a lie it kills you to know it's their truth,

That this particular person chose to say these things to you,

In that instant you feel your entire heart shatter,

Frantically trying to scoop up the pieces every time someone asks what's the matter,

But the fact is the actual words aren't what's hurting you,

It's the person who they came from and what that person chose to see in you,

ROCKY THE POET

If I were the crying type, I would have drowned in my own tears by now,

If I were the violent type I would be your biggest fear right now,

I can't believe the way you handled me,

The nerve of you to carry it like I'm just anybody,

Like I didn't love you when you were unlovable,

Or like I didn't grant you sole access to what was untouchable,

I gave you my heart and I waited for yours,

But after every level that I beat there was always more,

This is a never-ending battle for a world I was never going to get,

Paying for mistakes that I didn't commit,

Working against time and space,

Just to put a smile on your face,

Desperately trying to love away the hate,

Only to be constantly reminded that I can be replaced,

But by who? Who in the world is going to love you?

When you won't allow anyone to,

I struggled so hard to keep you together that I didn't see it was tearing me apart,

Out of all the things in the world to play with you chose my heart?

The one thing I never wanted to give you,

EXPOSED: MY WRITE TO LIVE

I don't know rather to feel angry or sorry for you,

Because sadly a piece of my soul still loves you,

But I'm done trying to save you from yourself,

If you don't care if you self-destruct why should anyone else,

I will deal with my hurt and heartaches and create a better me,

You will still be failing at love miserably,

I wish you the best but just give me back the best parts of me,

The time I wasted on a bitter soul that just was not worthy,

Now, now you get to watch me leave,

After days and nights of me begging you to stop mistreating me,

After tear-drenched pillows that were the only thing that was there to comfort me,

Now you want to do right by me,

Now you want to go to church,

Now you want to make it work,

Never mind the countless ways you've left me hurt,

Hurt, so hurt I couldn't wrap my brain around what I did to deserve it,

Hurting while trying to find the broken pieces of myself so I could preserve it,

Only to reach the end of you and realize you were never worth it,

Worth, I lost the true definition of mine when you added less,

ROCKY THE POET

Less honesty, less loyalty, but more stress,

I watched myself transform into this monster that fed only on anger,

Angry that what I entrusted you to keep safe you put in danger,

Angry that the person I use to be had now become a stranger,

Angry that when I looked in the mirror, I couldn't name her,

See you want to mention another man and well that is funny to me,

Funny because I never cheated on you instead, I only cheated me,

Funny that all the times I begged for your love you just couldn't see,

Funny that the person I'm actually leaving you for is none other than ME,

Because once she spoke of her love for me,

I knew for a fact me and you could never be,

So, while all others you may deceive,

You gonna have to grab a seat or stand,

I don't care if you understand, but YOU my friend, get to watch me leave!

ORGANIC CONFUSION

How did this happen?

How did I fall so unequivocally deep in love with someone who doesn't love me?

Someone who is unaffected by my tears, who is deaf to my cries,

Someone who is so comfortable in my truth while feeding me lies,

How the hell did this happen?

What the hell was I doing that I became blind,

Eyes focused on a bigger picture that you could never find,

Eyes crying from a pain that you don't seem to mind,

Eyes that you once thought were beautiful,

The same eyes that saw past your hurt, dirt, and bruised ego,

If you are waiting for me to call this some misguided jacked up mistake,

Keep waiting because my love was as intentional as your hate,

My love was as pure as the shit you couldn't seem to give,

My love was the foundation on which this relationship lived,

So, when you move on keep this in mind,

That as long as there is a foundation the rebuild will always be fine,

So, thank you for the tornado that is you that tore my world apart,

Because with my love as the foundation I'm granted a beautiful new start,

ROCKY THE POET

A recourse to correct the shattered mess that was me,

A rebuild to illuminate God's favor, love and glory, how did this happen?

How didn't I see, that this perfectly broken heart,

Was broken to get the best that God has for me!

MEN GET TIRED TOO

She didn't notice that he waited up for her to ensure her safety,

She failed to see that he paid the bills to ensure her a life of luxury,

She ignored his loving calls and text,

She even began to withhold sex,

She didn't see any reason to change,

She thought things would always remain the same,

But one day he woke up,

And something inside him was fed up,

He noticed she never said thank you,

He paid attention even when she thought he had no clue,

He was aware of everywhere she went,

And was hurt by who and where her time was spent,

Now correct me if I'm wrong but pay the bills around here,

Don't you dare shed a single tear,

I don't feel sorry for you,

Get your crap and get out my house, better yet let me help you,

I swore I thought I was going crazy so help me God!

I can't believe I fell for that good girl façade,

ROCKY THE POET

Oh, you thought you was slick?

To think of the way I trusted you makes me sick,

I would call you out your name, but my momma taught me better than that,

Oh, and I told her and my sisters what you did so I hope your "girls" got your back,

Where they at anyway tell them come help you,

The same ones who cover and lie for you!

Don't touch me, the damage is done,

Go on bout your life and see if you can find another one,

A man who is going to love you the way I did,

One who loves and accepts you and your kids,

Well your ride is here so go!

All the years I had you and have nothing to show,

Leave the ring on the table,

I'll find a worthy woman to wear it God able,

She didn't notice he had done all he could do,

Until he kissed her forehead and said baby, I'm leaving you.

QUEENDOM

She blew her fallen King the kiss of death,

She was bored of the girls he played with they were peasants at best,

She smiled as She whispered off with his head,

For this occasion, it seemed fitting to wear red,

Symbolizing her glorious freedom,

What could he be thinking, this was HER kingdom,

Before she gave the signal, she gently kissed his tear stained cheek,

I guess they should have told you NEVER TO MESS WITH ME,

His eyes widened as he begged for mercy,

She stood, smiled, and gave a curtsy,

She drew her finger across her neck sick of hearing his heavy breath,

Beautifully kissed her hand and blew him the kiss of death.

REFLECTIONS

Truth is I'm in love with you,

Beautiful, astonishing, insatiable you,

I couldn't always see your worth,

Now I know there isn't anyone like you in all the earth,

Yes, I'm quite taken with you,

Phenomenal, ravishing, exceptional you,

I've learned to appreciate who you are and who you're not,

The authenticity you possess could never be bought,

Oh, how I am so smitten with you,

Even private, loud, procrastinating you,

You didn't let your past define who you would become,

You challenged your environment and won... Baby who are you talking to?

I stood staring in the mirror and whispered...You!!!

I LOVE YOU

I love you, I love you, I love you,

I could speak this a thousand times,

It still would not come close to articulating what goes through my mind,

Full off your kisses so what's for dessert,

To be that sexy has got to be a blessing and a curse,

Your body is finger food, food my fingers take pleasure in,

To go without your love would leave me dry as the desert sand,

I love you, I love you, I love you,

Three little words I work overtime to express to you,

I never want you to question for a second,

If I appreciate you because you are my present,

A gift I'm not sure what I ever did right in my life to deserve,

I love you, you are God's most perfect work,

Delicious in all your ways,

To God be the glory and all the praise,

See Daddy when He made you, He broke the mold,

Said it is well with my soul,

And you are alright with me,

I love you, I love you, I love you, from now until the ends of eternity!

A MOTHER'S HEART

I can't wait to watch you grow to be everything you can possibly be,

You are beautiful, astonishing, and so intelligent, the very best parts of me,

I'd lose my life before I let harm come your way,

Forgive me please for my shortcomings each and every day,

You take my breath away you simply amaze me,

Everything you do and say to me is simply amazing,

The best gift was worth the price,

Only for you do I make this sacrifice,

You helped me in many ways and I'm forever grateful,

Just for your health and love I'm so very thankful,

God is real I know every time I see your delightful face,

Because you wouldn't be here and neither would I if not for His mercy and grace,

You turned this caterpillar into a glorious proud butterfly,

Who learned to trust her own wings and began to fly,

You made me something magnificent,

And as your mother I know you my angels are heaven sent.

MATRIMONY

I've pictured this moment all my life,

The moment we become husband and wife,

Not the day or the fancy things,

But the lifetime I get to spend with the man of my dreams,

The moment I decided to accept your blemished being,

And you decided to love my flaws without fleeing,

I promised to God to love you to the best of my abilities,

Rather it's chaos all around or we walk in perfect tranquilities,

In other words, for better or worse,

I vow to always be a blessing and never a curse,

May God convict me if I pick at you,

May I be reminded of why I fell in love with you,

This moment will lead to times we can't stand each other,

But let us declare to get through the best we can and try to come out better,

There shall be seconds that are harder than minutes that passed before,

And years that fly by, but our love will endure,

Our love will flourish because I'm never giving up on you,

And Because the love you provide is beautifully true,

ROCKY THE POET

But even in the ugliest of all moments we face,

I will not slander your name or celebrate the disgrace,

Instead I will seek God as I did when He sent you,

And recall the blessing for me, He created in you,

Instead I will search first my own soul for issues,

Forgive your shortcomings and decide to pray with you,

All I ask in return is that you match my effort even when I seem excruciating,

Because my heart, my life, and my hand are yours for the taking...

LASTING LOVE

He makes her laugh one of those mouth open, over the moon laughs,

And it's clear to all those watching that they are having a blast,

He kisses her cheek as they dance face to face,

She turns around, but he never breaks the embrace,

He sees no other woman but her the entire night,

Line after line, joke after joke, she bites,

They people watch, not realizing the people are watching them,

Wondering what he sees in her, or her in him,

He whispers in her ear,

She smiles and pulls him near,

His hand on the small of her back,

He kisses her again, this time she kisses him back,

Surprised by her touch, he steps back and smiles,

Silently hoping her interest compiles,

She imagines him being the love her life,

He still can't believe that she is his wife.

It was always you, you that I dreamed of,

When I dreamed dreams of real love,

ROCKY THE POET

You that I prayed for before I ever knew your name or saw your beautiful face,

I prayed that God would show you mercy and keep you safe,

I was praying you through storms long before you came into my life,

I didn't know you but somehow, I knew I was your wife,

And it was always you,

You were the reason no one else would ever do,

You are my living proof that dreams do come true,

I realize I didn't really know me until I met you,

And now it's clear that it was always you...

LOVING BY EXAMPLE

Sure as the sky is blue,

I will always love you,

I want to never for a second forget,

That your love is my perfect fit,

We will be challenged, we have been tested,

And we have overcome because negativity we've neglected,

As I sit here enjoying the comfort of your best,

There is an understanding that it is here I find rest,

Time passes and all things beautiful fade,

I quietly pray we can walk the path He has laid,

Like a storm, distractions clouded our clarity,

We began to question if this was love or charity,

Old hurts never snuck in because in you I trust,

We truly have forever, what's the rush,

You ask me how I need you, as if I have to explain,

I need you like we need the sun and flowers need rain,

You ask me how long I will love you,

I answer as long as there is breath inside of you,

You ask me when I look into your eyes what do I see,

ROCKY THE POET

I quickly reply, the very best part of me,

You question my feelings when all I'm trying to prove,

Is no matter the issues it can't change my love for you,

I'm lost in thought, thinking of you,

Knowing that after all these years I only have eyes for you,

Knowing that the battles fought were all worth it for you,

You may question my feelings but all I ever want to say,

Is that I love you more now, than yesterday,

This is a promise and a vow I'm here to stay,

No matter when, where, or how my love is never far away,

And when you ask me how I made you fall for me,

I will remind you, by giving you all of me,

And we will make it, we will be just fine,

Because this was God's plan, His perfect design.

YET I LOVE HIM

To put it simply, I love him,

Like my favorite love song, or my favorite hymn,

But even that definition fails in comparison, to what I feel for, him,

I love him, I am in love with him, from his dirty past to his bright future ahead,

From every mistake he made knowing that it was all God led,

From him laying beautifully or kneeling in prayer beside the bed,

I love him, I am in love with his scars,

Because they show me that he survived something harsh,

And he reminds me that without God he couldn't make it this far,

I love him, purely and entirely,

Because he's seen the worse in me,

Yet still chooses to reference only my beauty,

But still that's just a drop of my love for him,

I haven't even begun to speak on it,

On how no matter what was done this love I can't get rid of it,

Or how at the sight of his smile, all anger I forget,

My God I love him, and I don't want to at all,

I want to be mad and not answer his call,

But in his arms our issues seem small,

And there is no other place I'd rather be at all,

I could go on and on, but like I said I love him,

And all that comes with him,

I could be content with you and I'd still choose to be miserable with him,

Who wants to just be content anyway, and force a love that will not stay,

When no matter what you do or say,

I will still be thinking of him! I don't want to hurt you or anyone else,

But without him I'm hurting myself,

This isn't the kind of love you sit on a shelf,

It's the kind that won't leave you alone, the kind that won't ease,

The kind that brought Rome to its knees,

The kind God created just between him and me, and I love him...

BONUS MOM

Dear Honey,

I'm so sorry that you got dragged into bitterness it truly breaks my heart,

To count the days, the weeks, and the months we've been apart,

God knows the many times your dad and I have cried,

Hoping to see you and praying you see the truth no matter who lied,

Your siblings ask for you every day,

Wondering why your mom chooses to keep you away,

Your baby brother will be one next month and sadly hasn't seen you for half of his life,

I pray God soon ends this heartache and strife,

No matter what please know that you have a family that truly loves you,

And we will NEVER stop fighting for you,

Blood couldn't make our bond any more official,

Love always, your other mom with the same initials,

Dear Princess,

It is my greatest hope that you will always know,

That I will always be here for you to help you grow,

I'm honored that your dad chose me to be a part of your life,

ROCKY THE POET

And despite the chaos for you I'll always fight,

I will always adjust your crown and help you carry it if I have to,

I'm here to wipe your tears and be extra support for you,

Whatever you may come to doubt in this lifetime,

You'll never have to question this love of mine,

So, while there is so much I want to teach you,

I just enjoy the moments I get to see you,

I know you will do amazing things,

And I will always encourage you to follow your dreams,

I love you more with each passing day,

And will always help you find your way.

SOUL

GOD, I NEED A MOMENT

You ever have that unwelcomed, unscheduled, moment when you want to cry,

The lump in your throat, and you can't really say why,

That moment that over takes you out of nowhere,

The one that leaves you wondering does anyone care,

When you recognize that you pour so much into everyone else,

That maybe, just maybe you've lost sight of yourself,

That is the precise moment I'm talking about,

The one where you want to scream but nothing comes out,

You can't see through the constant stream of tears,

You are sobbing so loudly, and still no one hears,

That moment you feel invisible because those who matter most just don't see you,

Have you had that moment? Yea I have too,

But no worries because I know a man who has felt the same,

One who can make it all better just by the mention of His name,

He heals me every single time I have moments like these,

He's easy to reach just hit your knees...

Though I have not been discouraged just yet,

For I serve a God who paid it all, so I can have all I can get!

EXPOSED: MY WRITE TO LIVE

I have more to give, more than just some superficial life to live,

More than just some ratty used up thing,

Much, much more than just a dollar and a dream,

I have Him and He owns it all,

And in order to receive it I must answer His call,

Following man, I've often been deceived,

But following Him I've only been relieved,

Made better but still the same,

All at the mention of His name,

Transformed by the renewing of my mind,

And even as my heart aches, I know I'll be just fine,

For morning by morning new mercies I see,

And as He watches the sparrow, I know He's watching me,

And though He slay me, yet will I trust Him all the more,

Because no matter what I face He is my strength to endure,

Focused on today but working toward tomorrow,

Covered by His blood and free from sorrow.

MY PRAISE

Knowing I am nothing without Him is not just a song to sing,

But is a definition of my mess that to God I humbly bring,

Yeah, they are right it is a petition to God that I cannot argue,

Petition is just a pretty word for begging Him to forgive me for what I put Him through,

Yeah, I said it what I put Him through, because I ain't scared to admit I ain't as perfect as you,

I have backslid, back stroked, two-stepped, and attempted to twerk my way to hell,

But God, But God looked at me and saw Christ who died for me and said IT IS WELL!!!

Prayer did that, it was not any greatness of my own,

I'm standing here today on the prayers of grandmothers who went boldly before His throne,

See if you think for one second you are here because of you,

Then honey PLEASE allow me to reality check you,

Just think back for one second where'd you be without Him,

Recall the people you thought would always be there and try praying to them,

You see prayer is an intimate meeting between just you and God,

Worship Him in spirit and in truth leaving behind the phony façade,

Prayer releases healing, all we have to do is ask and believe,

The same miracles you read about in the Bible our God can still achieve...

SHADES OFF

As I sit here God showed me that I have been looking at my life through shades not because my future was bright,

But instead because I was afraid of the light,

Because I was mourning all I lost in the fight,

Because I was depressed about not getting it right,

So, He gently removed my shades and showed me the rainbow extended from His glory,

The rainbow after the rain He's showering down on me,

Gave me new sight to see a different perspective to tell my story,

To lift Him up while He draws all men unto me,

So, gather around and hear the tales of how I rose from the odds stacked against me,

All because I climbed up faith and looked beyond what my eyes could see,

He removed the shades, so I could see clearly,

Removed my shades so I couldn't hide from me,

Broke my shades to never again hide from the love He has for me...

REAL LOVE

You push me away, but I won't let go,

I'm here to restore you and your soul,

You turn your back on me, and walk away,

But I love you more, day by day,

I forgive you and wipe your slate clean,

Yet you say you don't have time for me,

WHAT DO YOU MEAN?

I give you one hundred percent though you never give it back,

Filling in wherever you ask so nothing you lack,

Though I am strong,

I have a weakness for you,

I've proven my love, giving my life a time or two,

I can pour you out a blessing you don't have room enough to receive,

But instead you try to trick me, and pimp me with broken promises; you deceive,

I am all knowing, that means I know it ALL,

While you judge others, to me no sin is too big or too small,

I'm here for you, loving you no matter what,

Yes, that is me, that nagging feeling deep down in your gut,

ROCKY THE POET

Don't be afraid, fear me not, for I am the reason you have all you got,

You push me away, but I will not let you go,

For I know the real you, and still I love your soul.

TIME

We all have a set time to leave this place,

This is a concept we all MUST face,

So, I ask what WILL you do,

When the time is UP for you,

When it is your turn to say GOODBYE,

And there's no more time for second tries,

How will you feel,

When things are left undone and there's no more time to heal,

Can you say that your life is what you wanted, and everything is great?

Or are there things you need to change before death seals your fate?

DEATH discriminates not,

Stop playing around and make the best of the time you got,

Your day is coming, please be certain of that,

So, think it over because once you're gone you can never come back,

Make amends and live in peace,

Instead of resting there or living in grief,

Do your best to be your best daily,

Shine your light as brightly as possible and stay away from anything shady,

ROCKY THE POET

What will you do,

When time is up for you,

Enjoy every breath,

Before you are laid to rest...

THANKFUL

Lord I am thankful for Your love and all that it gives,

I'm thankful that You took on my death so that I may live,

Lord I thank You for my beautiful bloodline,

I'm grateful for these stunningly beautiful, intelligent, children of mine,

I thank You for the women of classiness that I come from,

I'm grateful for the men of honor who taught me never to play dumb,

Lord I thank You for love and all the joy it brings,

So even when the world has silenced my lips, my heart still sings,

But Lord more than anything else, I thank You for life and the fullness thereof,

I am so grateful that my life is full of joy, peace, hurt, pain, ups, downs, kisses, tears,

And plenty of love…

BEYOND THE SURFACE

I hear it said all the time,

She's not THAT pretty and it blows my mind,

See if we are talking about physically then I'd have to agree,

Because to be honest there you will find nothing special about me,

But I must advise you that my beauty can't be seen with eyes,

Unless you are looking at the labors of my heart, that is where it lies,

Far past bone structure and skin,

The beauty you hear spoken about me comes from within,

I am not interested in those who are invested in my "beauty,"

But cannot, will not accept the real me,

If you only knew I'm not tripping off me,

 It's a whole lot of days I look in the mirror and don't like what I see,

Shoot, some days I feel and act ugly,

I even question why anyone would view me as "pretty",

This perplexes me,

Because I have stretch marks and my face is bumpy,

My stomach is soft, and my butt is lumpy,

So, I don't see anything amazing when I look at me,

At least not physically,

EXPOSED: MY WRITE TO LIVE

Now my heart? Now that's a different story,

Because truth be told no one will love you like me,

I will give whatever I have if you have a need,

If you're looking at my soul it is there you'll find beauty,

Because I gave it to God and He has rewarded me,

His Grace and Mercy, they follow me,

So, to be quite truthful and put it honestly,

This is why it is imperative that we not envy,

Because you never truly know someone else's story,

It is Him you admire when you look at me,

So, you can't see the way the world has crucified me,

Because He gave His Son to die for me,

Beyoncé said pretty hurts, but take it from me,

It only hurts when you create your own beauty.

ANGELS

I was once told a story of God's unchanging love,

It was said that He recruits special angels to assist Him high above,

Those who are so wonderful they make His heart delight,

That must have been the reason, I saw my angel take flight,

Every so often God allows a woman to become a mother to such a precious gift,

This woman carries an angel and gives birth to happiness,

I gave birth to an angel, though it was his love that gave life to me,

His little eyes saw my soul and loved me perfectly,

He changed my life in ways you will never know,

I carried him under my heart and now I carry him in my soul,

A very tiny presence had the greatest impact,

Although our time was short, I'll always remember that,

My heart aches just to smell your scent or see you smile,

But for you I live on, for you my precious angelic child,

I just want to say thank you for sharing your essence with me,

I am greater today all because I was your mommy,

My tears flow, and I won't stop them from falling,

Just as I could not stop you from answering God's calling,

EXPOSED: MY WRITE TO LIVE

I guess Grandma and Grandpa just couldn't wait to see you,

You are in good hands with so many others, who will be there to greet you,

We will love you forever and a day,

Although we desperately wish things were not this way,

Your memory will live on and inspire,

After all that is God's design and desire,

So, I guess the story is true,

Because I gave birth to an angel, the day He breathed life into you.

CHANGING PERSPECTIVES

Today is a new day, how many times have we spoken these words,

Unfortunately, this has become more like an adjective and less like a verb,

We negate to see the beauty in the fact that we've once again opened our eyes,

We are too focused on rushing through the work week to truly realize,

We do the same thing day in and day out, it's become mundane,

Never pausing to inhale life, instead we are waiting to exhale, this is insane,

It is ridiculous that we don't tell people how we feel until they are no longer with us,

Then they become our profile picture and we tell them with a Facebook status,

A status they will never read and emptiness we can't escape,

Today is a new day, embrace it before it's too late,

Today I choose to live with every fiber of my being,

Asking God for a new perspective on a life I hadn't been seeing,

Petitioning Him to show me how to use every morsel of talent He's given me,

Because I refuse to die without having used it all completely,

I refuse to sit when I've been required to stand,

EXPOSED: MY WRITE TO LIVE

I will march forward even when I don't understand,

I shall live, truly live my life,

In a manner in which God knows I am grateful for His sacrifice,

I am honored He sent His Son to die for me,

And I must live my life the way He promised me...

A GLORY MOMENT

I remember weeping and a man walking up to me,

Saying I'm a special man you should get to know me,

He spoke of His father as if He were a king,

As He spoke, I felt so good I thought it was a dream,

He was a beautiful man though I never seen His face,

His skin was so golden that I couldn't distinguish His race,

When I touched Him, it was like touching a cloud,

This phenomenal man made even a girl like me feel proud,

He told me that He knew what it felt like to cry,

And that His Father could heal my brokenness if I gave Him a try,

So, I asked is your Father a doctor?

And He answered no He is a Potter,

Then He pointed to His heart, said there I'd always have a home,

He told me that His Father is with me, so I should never feel alone,

Then He hugged me, and I felt every burden go away,

And it was then I realized that I gave my life to Jesus on that day.

I reflected on my broken past,

All the failed relationships that didn't last,

EXPOSED: MY WRITE TO LIVE

How often I was left all alone,

And never took it to the throne,

I was left empty and battered,

Left with a dream crushed and shattered,

I was left crying my eyes out,

Left to wallow in fear and self-doubt,

Left by the ones who were supposed to love me like no other,

Left by the ones I call father and mother,

Left, four little letters that have greatly impacted my life,

Left to wonder if I will ever recover from the heartache and strife,

Left to deal with this hurt and pick up the pieces,

Left to wonder if this empty feeling ever ceases,

Left to try to date again,

Left to pray and hope you understand,

Left to accept trash because that is all that was given to me,

Left to go above and beyond just because people see me,

Left to face the reality that you too will leave,

Left to wear my heart on my sleeve,

Left once again crying,

Left to stop myself from emotionally dying,

Left to care more when I rather careless,

ROCKY THE POET

Left to put my faith in God to the test,

Left to let it go and get over the hurt,

Left to pick myself up and give God my dirt,

Left to never be left again,

Left alone with God who will bring me to an expected end,

So, I leave my abandonment with you Lord,

Because with you I will never be left alone anymore.

WE NEED YOU

Sons are laying in their mothers' lap left to die,

Fathers who turn deaf ears to their pleading cry,

Fathers who choose to deal with the devil instead of what's right,

Sons left alone to blindly fight, Fatherless sons lost in that same role,

Son-less fathers turning the world cold, I see women with issues of blood,

Chasing behind mothers who are too weak to weather the flood,

Mothers who don't deserve to bear the name,

Mothers who leave their children to chase the game,

Motherless daughters craving attention,

Daughter-less mothers seeking the same need I mention,

Fathers left struggling to show their girls the way,

Daughters not willing to hear a word he says,

Heal our land Lord and our people,

Humble us Lord rebuke our ego's,

Let each one reach one and bring them all to you,

Do for us what no other could possibly do...

BATTERED BUT NOT BROKEN

Open my eyes blinking to try to regain my vision,

Feeling like I was just in a collision,

I can't see through my right eye and the left is full of blood,

I struggle to get up out of the mud,

I yell out someone answer the phone,

Only to realize the ringing is in my ears and I'm here all alone,

My lips are tight I know they are swollen again,

I feel for my phone to call the police on him,

Then I remember I didn't change my dress,

It is my fault I'm the cause of his stress,

He hits me because he loves me, I keep forgetting that,

So, love is responsible for this brutal attack,

Love is the reason I'm battered, black, and blue,

But I can never show this kind of love to you?

Just then a voice whispered No, Daughter it is all a lie,

I love you and I count every tear you cry,

I love you and for you I gave my life,

I was beaten and bruised so you'd never have to fight,

My love heals while His causes you pain,

He lies when he tells you he loves you and swears in my name,

You are worth more than this my child and I give you the strength to walk away,

But I love you enough to respect your free will and cover you if you choose to stay...

RELATIONSHIP OVER RELIGION

I knew You, I knew You before I ever knew religion,

So, loving You Lord was never a hard decision,

See I don't expect them to understand my love for You,

Because they don't know You like I do,

They weren't there the night they threw that bomb on our porch,

Being just four years old I watched my bedroom being completely torched,

Yet it was You who got me out without a single mark,

See it was that night, and that fire, that started the spark,

In that moment I felt my first real connection to You,

At that moment I began a relationship with You,

I used to beg my brother to sing Silent Night to me,

Back then I didn't know why that song would comfort me,

Now I realize that it was the closest thing to gospel us ghetto kids knew,

It was the only way at 4 years old I had to draw close to You,

Our relationship was founded rock solid the day our house was shot up,

Because I knew You were our shield and It wasn't just luck,

I knew then at age 6 someone greater than us was there,

And again at 7 when I lost my Nana, the one whose heart I share,

I knew You, I knew You before any corrupted skewed version of You was ever presented to me,

I knew You deep down in my soul to be the Prince of Peace!

Then we had a formal introduction at The Place Where the Lord Provides,

The first church I attended and felt like so this is where He resides,

I fell so deep into prayer everyone thought I was asleep,

Imagine my surprise when I found myself spiritually at Your feet,

It was the most majestic feeling in the world,

At 8 years old I finally found a father to love this broken little girl,

My GOD I KNEW YOU,

And without hesitation You knew me too!

I am not controlled by any man-made doctrine,

But bound by the unadulterated fellowship I have with Him,

So, I'm sorry I'm not interested in religious debaters or superficial views of Him,

I'm not swayed by those who decided to take the words of GOD and misuse them,

I don't serve You merely because of a religion that was forced on me,

I knew you before I was ever introduced to Christianity,

To put it simply you can't make me doubt Him,

I know too much about Him,

ROCKY THE POET

So, in life's biggest storms I can still find peace,

Close my eyes, relax my mind, and sleep,

Because I know him, fully and entirely,

Have you met my God, the force behind what inspires me,

He is my best friend and constant hope for tomorrow,

I know for a fact that He is my joy in sorrow,

You are entitled to your views and opinions, I won't question them,

But you won't ever shake my faith in God because I Know Him

Acknowledgments

I thank and give all glory to God for making this possible. I am proof that if you put your faith in Him and trust Him, He will give you the desires of your heart. I watched Him order every step and He led me to Vision to Fruition who took my dream and made it a reality thank you! To my amazing mother thank you for always giving me more love and support than I can handle. Thank you and Dad for giving your time, patience, two cents, and money just to get me here today I appreciate you both. To my husband thank you for holding my hand and my heart through this entire process I wouldn't have done this without you Papi you are the best! To my girls Boo, Jo, and Vonne thank you ladies for investing in my dream, encouraging me, helping me, and most importantly just being there for me whenever and however I needed. I love and appreciate you ladies and couldn't have done this without you. To my wonderful kids, thank you for showing me my own strength and giving me a determination, I wouldn't have if it weren't for you. You guys are my drive and reason to work harder. Thank you to everyone who ever offered any encouragement while I've been on this journey, you have no idea how much of a blessing your support and kind words have been to my life. Lastly thank you for buying this book and making a dream come true! God bless you all.

About the Author

Rocky began writing around the age of 10 as a way to cope with difficult situations. She has always had a love for the arts as well as English. Out of those two emerged her greatest passion -poetry. Rocky classifies herself as your everyday woman, she is a wife, mother, daughter, sister, and friend to many. The vast roles Rocky plays grant her the motivation and inspiration to write. Rocky's motto is - "I want it all for the price of my story, and none of it at all if God doesn't get the glory." Rocky has never been one to conform to the 'rules' of society which is evident in her work, but she wants to challenge the reader to see things from a different perspective. Rocky's work showcases a variety of issues and perspectives offering readers a clear understanding of who she is and what she stands for. Rocky believes that poetry has become her ministry often stating that "God speaks, I write." This is her first published work but certainly will not be her last.

About the Publisher

At Vision to Fruition, we are dedicated to helping others bring their personal, business, ministry & nonprofit visions to fruition.

Whether it's as grand as a book you want to write, a business you want to start, a conference or event you want to host, a ministry you want to launch or an organization you want to start; or as small as needing a computer repair, logo design or web design; Vision to Fruition will help you walk through the process and set you up for success! At Vision to Fruition we don't have clients, we have Visionaries. We provide solutions to equip others to pursue their visions & dreams with reckless abandon.

In 2018 we have published twenty-four authors, eight of which were Amazon Bestsellers. We would love for you to join our family of Visionaries as well!!!

Learn more here www.vision-fruition.com